RELEASE
YOUR
ANOINTING

STUDY
GUIDE

OTHER BOOKS BY T.D. JAKES

Why? Because You Are Anointed

Why? Because You Are Anointed Workbook

Can You Stand to Be Blessed?

Woman, Though Art Loosed!

Naked and Not Ashamed

Help Me, I've Fallen and I Can't Get Up!

Water in the Wilderness

The Harvest

The Harvest Workbook

AVAILABLE FROM DESTINY IMAGE PUBLISHERS

RELEASE
YOUR
ANOINTING
STUDY
GUIDE

Tapping the Power of the Holy Spirit in You

T.D. JAKES

Compiled by Jan Sherman.

DESTINY IMAGE® PUBLISHERS, INC.

P.O. Box 310, Shippensburg, PA 17257-0310

"Speaking to the Purposes of God for this Generation and for the Generations to Come."

This book and all other Destiny Image, Revival Press, Mercy Place, Fresh Bread, Destiny Image Fiction, and Treasure House books are available at Christian bookstores and distributors worldwide.

For a U.S. bookstore nearest you, call 1-800-722-6774.

For more information on foreign distributors, call 717-532-3040.

Reach us on the Internet: www.destinyimage.com.

ISBN 10: 0-7684-2655-3

ISBN 13: 978-0-7684-2655-7

For Worldwide Distribution, Printed in the U.S.A.

1 2 3 4 5 6 7 8 9 10 11 / 11 10 09 08

CONTENTS

DAY 1

HUMANKIND IS BODY, SOUL, AND SPIRIT

And I pray God your whole spirit and soul and body be pre-served blameless unto the coming of our Lord Jesus Christ (1 Thessalonians 5:23).

Excerpt: *Release Your Anointing*, Chapter 1.

This Scripture shows the three parts of humankind: body, soul, and spirit. If we want to have a successful prayer life and reach our full potential with God, each of these parts must be understood.

All three affect our prayer life. If we were only spirit, the blessings of prayer would be unrestrained, without hindrance. But we also have to deal with our body and soul.

The words *wholly* and *preserved* are significant. *Wholly* means to completely, absolutely reach the limit or potential. *Preserved* means to guard, to watch, to keep an eye on, to keep something in its place. As we pray, we must contend with these three parts.

1. Body

This entails our flesh and its appetites. The flesh never wants to pray.

2. Soul

The soul is sandwiched between our body, which never wants to pray or do right, and our spirit, which desires God and spiritual things. The soul entails our emotions, feelings, weaknesses, and our past.

3. Spirit

Now that you are saved, your spirit has been quickened. As the Holy Ghost begins to have an intimate relationship with our spirit, we begin to produce the "fruit of the Spirit" (Gal. 5:22-23).

Your Thoughts

1. If you were to explain the three parts of humankind to someone who does not know biblical terms, what would you say? To your understanding, how do these three parts work together?

_____

_____

_____

_____

2. What does First Thessalonians 5:23 mean to you?
    What does *blameless* mean to you? Do you believe you
    can be "blameless"?

    _____

    _____

    _____

3. In what way does your body participate in prayer?
    Why do you think it is so resistant to prayer? In
    what ways do you have to make the body submit to
    discipline?

    _____

    _____

4. In what way does your soul participate in prayer?
    How do you think your soul bridges between the
    body and the spirit? What part of your soul seems
    the most unruly or challenging to tame?

    _____

    _____

    _____

5. In what way does your spirit participate in prayer? How does the Holy Spirit commune with a person's spirit? What are the results that you have seen from this type of communion?

_____

_____

_____

_____

_____

_____

Meditation

"Apostle Paul wrote, 'that I may know Him' (Phil. 3:10), which implies a close relationship—one that causes us to partake in His experiences. But you can't know Christ in resurrection power until you know Him in His sufferings and death. Our old man must be crucified with Him daily as we are being changed from glory to glory."

What do you think Paul meant by wanting to "know" Christ? How well do you know Christ? How much do you participate in His sufferings and death as well as His resurrection power?

DAY 2

HELP IN PRAYER

Likewise the Spirit also helpeth our infirmities: for we know not what we should pray for as we ought: but the Spirit itself maketh intercession for us with groanings which cannot be uttered. And He that searcheth the hearts knoweth what is the mind of the Spirit, because He maketh intercession for the saints according to the will of God (Romans 8:26-27).

Excerpt: *Release Your Anointing*, Chapter 1.

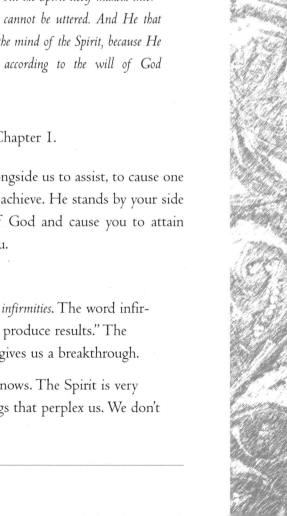

The Holy Ghost stands alongside us to assist, to cause one to stand, to cause one to achieve. He stands by your side to plead the covenant of God and cause you to attain what the covenant provides for you.

He does this in four ways:

1. He assists us through our *infirmities*. The word infirmities means "inability to produce results." The Holy Ghost helps us and gives us a breakthrough.

2. He assists us in that He knows. The Spirit is very knowledgeable about things that perplex us. We don't

always know what is right. He begins to tell us how to pray for certain things.

3. He assists us with intercessions. "He maketh intercession for us." Intercession means that the Holy Ghost will meet with us. He comes into our situation and speaks into our spirit as one who interviews another.

4. He assists us with Heaven's language. The Spirit pleads the will of God to us. As creation groans, it speaks a language that only God can interpret.

The Holy Ghost is one with God. He will never speak anything that is not sanctioned by the Word.

Your Thoughts

1. Have you ever experienced the Holy Ghost assisting you in some area that you felt you could not do on your own? What part does the Holy Ghost play in assisting us in prayer?

_____

_____

_____

_____

2. Have you ever experienced the Holy Ghost helping you stand when you felt you would fall down either spiritually, emotionally, mentally, or physically? How does the Holy do this kind of work for us?

    _____

    _____

3. Have you ever experienced the Holy Ghost helping you to achieve something that seemed out of reach in your own power? How does the Holy Spirit make a difference in these types of situations?

    _____

    _____

4. Look through the list of four ways God assists us. How is each of these areas important to us personally if we are to grow into Christ's likeness or bring glory to God?

    _____

    _____

    _____

5. How does the Oneness of the Holy Ghost with the
Father bring credibility to what the Holy Spirit does?
How does this resemble what Jesus said about what
He did while on earth?

_____

_____

_____

_____

Meditation

In John 16:13, Jesus said the Holy Ghost would do four things:

1. Guide you into all truth.

2. Speak truth to you, but not speak of Himself.

3. Show you all truth concerning things to come.

4. Speak into you what He hears Heaven speaking.

We must be able to hear what He is saying. But it is equally
important to know the Holy Ghost hears what to speak to us.

Think through the four things listed. Have you experienced
each of these personally? Why do you think it is so important to
know that the Holy Spirit does not compose His own words to us?

DAY 3

BUILD UP YOURSELF

But ye, beloved, building up yourselves on your most holy faith, praying in the Holy Ghost, keep yourselves in the love of God, looking for the mercy of our Lord Jesus Christ unto eternal life. And of some have compassion, making a difference: And others save with fear, pulling them out of the fire; hating even the garment spotted by the flesh (Jude 20-23).

Excerpt: *Release Your Anointing*, Chapter 1.

The word *build* is an architectural word that means "to cause a building to stand." It means "to lay a good foundation." In the natural realm, it is always important to leave yourself the ability to add on to your building in case you need to expand in the future. If you have outgrown your spiritual house, the Holy Ghost gives you the resources to add on to meet your demands.

Are there weak areas in the structure? Build them up. You do this by praying in the Holy Spirit.

God leads you through a progressive path, but the ultimate goal is to be fruitful. Like Elijah, He wants you to be able to call

fire down from Heaven, to see into the Spirit, and to persevere in prayer until God intervenes in your situation. The answer to your drought may appear to be a cloud the size of a man's hand, but you know a refreshing rain is about to fall.

This is why Christians from all denominations are being filled with the Holy Ghost. Having outgrown the tradition of their past experiences, they have passed the tests and are ready for fruitfulness.

Your Thoughts

1. Think through Jude 20-23 and consider the impact of the words on your life. Do you regularly obey the admonitions contained in the verses?

   _____

   _____

2. How are we to build a good foundation for our spiritual house? What are the elements of a good foundation?

   _____

   _____

   _____

3. Do you think you have outgrown your spiritual house? How can you tell? What signs are there that God wants you to have more?

_____

_____

_____

4. How does the progressive path God gives us allow us to take steps forward without stumbling? How can we recognize this path so we continue to move forward instead of standing still without motion?

_____

_____

_____

5. Why do we need to get rid of traditions in order to progress in God? Do you have any traditions that you need to leave behind in order to move forward to fruitfulness?

_____

_____

Meditation

If you feel a hunger to go on with God, the Holy Ghost is telling you that your current spiritual house is too small. He is urging you to build on your foundation. In order to do this, however, we must pray in the Holy Ghost.

Where is your spiritual house? What does it mean that it is "too small"? Take time to ask the Lord to build on your foundation. Take time to pray in the Holy Ghost.

DAY 4

MORE BENEFITS OF PRAYING IN TONGUES

What is it then? I will pray with the spirit, and I will pray with the understanding also: I will sing with the spirit, and I will sing with the understanding also (I Corinthians 14:15).

Excerpt: *Release Your Anointing*, Chapter I.

Unlike giving a message in tongues in a public meeting, which edifies other people, *praying* in tongues edifies you.

Praying in tongues does at least five things for you individually:

1. Praying in tongues gives you the ability to talk to God alone, frustrating the devil. Praying in tongues enables you to bypass satan's radar system.

2. Praying in tongues edifies the person praying. As you pray in tongues, you enlarge your borders.

3. Praying in tongues helps you put on the armor of God. This armor dresses you for any occasion.

4. Praying in tongues builds up a wall of defense. The Holy Spirit stands by as your ally.

5. Praying in tongues helps you relieve anxiety. Praying in the Spirit allows you to *come apart* before you *come apart*. Like Jesus, you need a solitary place to rest awhile.

That's why we need to pray within the spirit realm, which is bigger than any problem, weakness, or dilemma we face. We also need to ask God to interpret to us the things that we have spoken through the auspice of the Holy Ghost. As He reveals them to us, we will gain understanding.

Your Thoughts

1. How does praying in tongues give you the ability to bypass satan and talk to God alone? How does it frustrate the devil?

_____

_____

_____

_____

_____

2. Define *edify* in your own words. How does praying in tongues edify you? What does it mean to "enlarge your borders"? Have you enlarged your borders?

_____

_____

_____

3. Can you name the pieces of the armor of God that are mentioned in Ephesians 6? How does praying in tongues help you dress yourself in these pieces of armor? How does this make us ready for whatever happens?

_____

_____

4. How does praying in tongues help us build up a wall of defense? What kind of defense is made on your behalf? How does the Holy Spirit become your ally?

_____

_____

5. In what way does praying in tongues help to relieve your anxiety? How does this help you get away from earthly cares and distractions?

_____

_____

_____

_____

_____

_____

Meditation

"Praying in the Spirit pulls us into an experience with God. It's not surprising that Paul wondered whether he was in the body or out of the body. The apostle saw and heard things unlawful for a man to speak. God in the Spirit takes us to paradise, pulling us apart from the pressures of the world before we are pulled apart."

Have you ever felt spiritually blah, but after praying in the Spirit, felt pulled into an experience with God? What benefits of paradise could you use right now?

DAY 5

WE NEED THE ANOINTING

Wherefore seeing we also are compassed about with so great a cloud of witnesses, let us lay aside every weight, and the sin which doth so easily beset us, and let us run with patience the race that is set before us (Hebrews 12:1).

Excerpt: *Release Your Anointing*, Chapter 1.

Sometimes we don't know what to say. Our hearts are crushed; our spirits are overwhelmed. We know that we need a touch. We know the area that needs to be touched, but we don't always know what to say.

Have you ever been so overwhelmed, so overcome that all you can do is groan? Maybe you can only say, "Jesus, help me," or "I need You, Lord." That's when we need to change our language. We need to wait on the Holy Ghost because He knows how to pray—and what to pray. The Holy Ghost will always pray in alignment with the will of God (Rom. 8:27).

In these last days, satan and all his cohorts are waging a final onslaught against the Church. We must know God in a way in

which we have never known Him before. Within you are miracles, unborn babies, ministries, and gifts. We all have callings.

Your Thoughts

1. The anointing brings power. How can you tap into that power to overcome the enemy's attacks?

    _____

    _____

    _____

    _____

2. God shows Himself in the holy of holies (Exod. 25:17-22). Have you been there? Has He revealed Himself to you as promised? If not, why do you think that is?

    _____

    _____

    _____

3. What miracles do you think are within you? How is satan keeping you from birthing those miracles?

_____

_____

_____

4. Scripture tells us "the gifts and callings of God are without repentance" (Rom. 11:29). You can release your anointing when you can see the raw, undiluted presence of God. Are you actively looking for Him?

_____

_____

_____

5. Have you allowed satan to veil your mind to God's presence because of past failures or experiences? What can you do to unveil the beauty within?

_____

_____

_____

Meditation

"The anointing of the Holy Ghost doesn't always bring chills or goosebumps. It isn't always charged with emotion.... You need to get to where you can see the raw, undiluted presence of God and His anointing. Only then can you release your anointing to bring glory to His Kingdom."

Are you afraid to give total control of your life, spirit, soul, body to the Holy Ghost? What is the worse-case scenario that you can imagine if you did give Him total control? What is the best-case scenario that you can imagine? Choose today.

DAY 6

YOU CAN RECEIVE THE HOLY GHOST

And I will pray the Father, and He shall give you another Comforter, that He may abide with you forever (John 14:16).

Excerpt: *Release Your Anointing*, Chapter 2.

You have the right to receive the Holy Ghost because Jesus prayed for you to receive Him.

The Holy Ghost has been given to assist us in a variety of ways. He helps to guide us (John 16:13). He assures us that we are children of God (Rom. 8:16). He gives us power to witness (see Acts 1:8). He helps us to pray (Rom. 8:26). He enables us to bear the fruit of the Spirit (Gal. 5:22-23).

The Holy Ghost is always present. He is our backup! The Holy Ghost stands by the children of God to assist them in carrying out the same work—and even "greater works" (see John 14:12). Believers must understand the ministry of the Holy Ghost so they can carry out the will of God for their lives.

We aren't alone when we lie down at night or go through the storms of life. When we go through a valley or through a trial, the Holy Ghost is there to defend us. When we receive the fullness of the Holy Ghost, we receive an eternal friend. Jesus is praying that you have an intimate relationship with the Holy Ghost.

Your Thoughts

1. If Jesus prayed that we would receive the Holy Ghost, does this make the act of receiving Him optional or mandatory? Why do you think it is so important that we receive this part of the Trinity?

_____

_____

2. Have you seen the Holy Ghost's assistance in your life or in the life of others around you in the following areas: guidance; assurance; witnessing; prayer; bearing fruit? How can you tell if it is the Holy Spirit who is assisting the believer?

_____

_____

3. Why is the Holy Spirit so important to our ministry on earth? What does the Holy Spirit do to enable us to carry out the will of the Father?

    _____

    _____

4. Has the Holy Ghost's presence been made real to you in any specific way in terms of your life experiences? If so, relate an incident or events that demonstrated His presence. If not, what do you think His presence would be like?

    _____

    _____

5. What do you think it means to be an "eternal friend" of the Holy Ghost? What would characterize an "intimate relationship" with Him?

    _____

    _____

Meditation

"Many friends stay with us until we mess up or until we disagree with them. They quickly leave as if they never knew us. But the Holy Ghost, our Comforter, stays with us forever. The Holy Ghost does not come and go based on the circumstances of our lives. In the same way that Jesus helped the disciples, the Holy Ghost now helps us."

Since the Holy Ghost does not abandon us when we are in trouble or sin, what do we need to do to depend on His friendship in the midst of trials? What do you think it takes for us to become more dependent on Him than on ourselves when we mess up?

DAY 7

WHEN DO WE
RECEIVE THE HOLY GHOST?

And, behold, I send the promise of My Father upon you: but tarry ye in the city of Jerusalem, until ye be endued with power from on high (Luke 24:49).

Excerpt: *Release Your Anointing,* Chapter 2.

God's Word shows that a person receives the Holy Ghost as a mark of identity, confirming that he or she really is a child of God (see John 3:5-6; Rom. 8:9,14-16; Gal. 4:6).

The apostle Paul commanded the Ephesian believers to "be filled with the Spirit" (Eph. 5:18). They had already been saved by the grace of God (Eph. 2:8-9), and had been sealed by the Holy Ghost (Eph. 1:13).

Despite these things, apostle Paul admonished them to be filled with the Holy Ghost.

In order for the Ephesians to be happy and bold, to walk in the will of God, to talk in a new way, and not be afraid of their future, they needed to be filled with the Holy Ghost.

Ephesians closes with a discussion of the battle that we face as children of God. If we are to partake of the blessings that God has predestined for us; if we are to be the workmanship of God; if we are to enjoy a happy marriage and rear children in the fear and admonition of the Lord; we will face a spiritual battle. Living a Spirit-filled life, however, abundantly equips us to carry out these tasks.

Your Thoughts

1. How do you think that receiving the Holy Ghost gives a believer a "mark" of identity? Is this mark a visible sign? How do you think this identity is perceived by others?

_____

_____

_____

2. When we are saved by grace, how does the Holy Spirit woo us to the cross of Christ? How is this different than being filled with the Spirit?

_____

_____

_____

3. What benefits does the believer have when filled with the Holy Spirit? Have you personally experienced any of the benefits you named?

_____

_____

_____

4. Why do you think the Holy Spirit is such a necessary part of walking in the will of God? What kind of difference do you think the Holy Spirit makes so we can fulfill God's will?

_____

_____

5. How dramatic has the Holy Spirit been in your own life in terms of your family relationships, the blessings you have received, the challenges you have faced, the battles you have won, and the fulfillment of the destiny God has worked within you?

_____

_____

Meditation

You can be saved, but not necessarily filled or baptized with the Holy Ghost. We receive the Holy Ghost as a mark of identity when we are saved, but another experience—the baptism in the Holy Ghost—awaits us. The believers in Acts 10:44-46 and Acts 19:1-7 had not been baptized in or received the infilling of the Holy Ghost. Peter and Paul found it necessary to address this.

Do you see any difference between Christians who have received salvation and those who have gone on to receive the baptism of the Holy Spirit? Is there a distinction in your life so people can tell the difference the Holy Spirit has made in you? Are you "visibly" marked?

DAY 8

WE MUST *SEEK*
WHAT WE ASK FOR

And I say unto you, Ask, and it shall be given you; seek, and ye shall find; knock, and it shall be opened unto you. For every one that asketh receiveth; and he that seeketh findeth; and to him that knocketh it shall be opened (Luke 11:9-10).

Excerpt: *Release Your Anointing,* Chapter 2.

Jesus said that those who seek shall find. Jesus wants us to desire the Holy Ghost. Would you ask for something and have your head or hand turned the other way? Jesus wants our hearts to be lined up with what our lips are saying.

Jesus taught this parable:

…what woman having ten pieces of silver, if she lose one piece, doth not light a candle, and sweep the house, and seek diligently till she find it? And when she hath found it, she calleth her friends and her neighbours together, saying, Rejoice with me; for I have found the piece which I had lost (Luke 15:8-9).

When this woman realized she didn't have her precious coin, she lit a candle, swept the house, and searched diligently until she found it. We must be in the same place of earnest seeking in regard to the Holy Ghost.

We must sweep our house and purge ourselves of anything that isn't of God. Then we must seek the Holy Ghost diligently. We must earnestly want the Holy Ghost and refuse to compromise. You can be real and have the Holy Ghost. It isn't something mysterious. This is God's will for your life!

Your Thoughts

1. What has Luke 11:9-10 meant to you personally? What have you sought for spiritually? What have you found that gives meaning to these words?

_____

_____

_____

_____

_____

2. Have you ever lost something valuable and become
    determined to continue looking until you found it?
    What makes the lost object worth the struggle and
    time to find it? Is the Holy Ghost this valuable to you?

    _____

    _____

    _____

3. Why do you think people often ask for something
    and turn away before receiving it? What position do
    we need to be in so we receive the blessings of God,
    including the Holy Spirit?

    _____

    _____

4. What counsel would you give someone who wanted
    to know how to receive the baptism of the Holy
    Ghost? What can you share from your personal expe-
    rience? What can you share from the principles in
    Scripture?

    _____

    _____

5. In your opinion, how does diligence come to play in regard to seeking the Holy Spirit? What kinds of compromise could we entertain so we do not really receive the Holy Spirit?

_____

_____

_____

_____

_____

_____

Meditation

"God rewards those who diligently seek Him (Heb. 11:6). _Diligently_ means to be stretched out for that which you are asking. The Holy Ghost, His power, and the change that He alone can bring in your life must be so precious that you will not accept a counterfeit. Nothing else will suffice."

Is your heart focused with a desire that will not take no for an answer? Do you really want the power of the Holy Ghost?

DAY 9

YOU HAVE TO KNOCK!

If ye then, being evil, know how to give good gifts unto your children: **how much more** *shall your heavenly Father give the Holy Spirit to them that ask Him?* (Luke 11:13).

Excerpt: *Release Your Anointing*, Chapter 2.

Those who want the power of the Holy Ghost must take a three-step approach: *ask, seek,* and *knock.* What prompts you to open your front door? When someone knocks, you see who it is and what they want.

Jesus said to knock. Before knocking, you must have a desire to ask. This driving desire caused you to come to the door with great expectation and determination. You searched until you found the door—and now you knock.

It may seem that Jesus has these steps out of order, but that's not true. If you have no will to ask, there's no reason to knock. Without the will to seek, there's no reason to knock. Knocking is preceded by a will to ask and search diligently. Knocking gives you access to what you have diligently sought.

An earthly father can be very biased. Sometimes he is stubborn, and sometimes he gives for all the wrong reasons. Jesus made it very clear: If the child asks for one thing, the Father will not give another.

The emphasis in Luke 11:13 (see above) is on "how much more."

Take the Word as authoritative—ask, seek, knock.

Your Thoughts

1. The author describes a three-step approach to receiving the power of the Holy Ghost. Think through each of the steps and define them in terms of your own knowledge and experience.

    _____

    _____

2. How does your desire to ask for the Holy Ghost precede your coming to God to "knock" for His empowerment? How much does asking have to do with your attitude and eagerness to receive?

    _____

    _____

    _____

3. How is your will involved in the three steps of asking, seeking, and knocking? What does a person's will have to do with the determination to receive?

_____

_____

_____

_____

4. If children ask for something good that is within your power to give, do you find it pleasurable and easy to give them what they ask? Why does it please us to give to a youngster? How does this example show us why the Father seeks to give blessings to us?

_____

_____

_____

_____

5. Explain Luke 11:13 in your own words, emphasizing the experience that you have with the progression explained in the verse. What are some things God may want you to ask, seek, and knock for right now?

_____

_____

_____

_____

_____

Meditation

"God knows that we need the power of the Holy Ghost. Spiritual gifts function only as the Holy Ghost empowers the child of God. As you ask and seek, remember that God knows your motives. He endues you with the power of the Holy Ghost to give you victory over satan, to make you joyful, and to enable you to function in the gifts of the Spirit."

Why do spiritual gifts only function when the Holy Ghost empowers us? Have you experienced this type of empowerment? Do you operate in it on a daily basis?

DAY 10

THE POWER AND ARMY OF THE HOLY GHOST

The wind bloweth where it listeth, and thou hearest the sound thereof, but canst not tell whence it cometh, and whither it goeth: so is every one that is born of the Spirit (John 3:8).

Excerpt: *Release Your Anointing*, Chapter 2.

The power of the Holy Spirit can make you everything God said you could be. Adam illustrates this perfectly. The Bible says that Adam as only a form until God breathed on him (Gen. 2:7). Only then did Adam become a living soul.

Until God breathed on him Adam had potential but no power. God breathed into Adam the power to reach his potential. The mere form of man became a living soul.

And suddenly there came a sound from Heaven as of a rushing mighty wind, and it filled all the house where they were sitting (Acts 2:2).

You have great potential. With great potential comes great responsibility. God has shaped you, but you need His power to become everything He desires for you to become. Without the power of the Holy Ghost you can go to Heaven, but you will never reach your potential. Your ministry, gifts, calling, life, and your marriage will be only a form of what it could have been.

Without a word from God the valley of dry bones that Ezekiel saw would have never been raised to form an army.

Look at the principles from Ezekiel 37:

1. You must be willing to confess your condition.

2. You must confess that you are merely a form of what you could be.

3. You must hear the Word of God.

4. The Word will bring about change.

5. The potential will be realized as the Word brought about the wind.

Your Thoughts

1. Have you felt God's mighty wind in your life? If your life is calm, where do you think God can stir it up with His breath of life?

_____

_____

2. In the busyness of your days, do you take enough time to feel His cool breeze of refreshment? What steps can you take to set aside time to walk in His presence?

_____

_____

3. Do you sense hidden potential within your spirit? Is there a career or ministry that seems "right" for you to pursue? What's holding you back?

_____

_____

_____

4. Do you ever feel powerless regarding family situations, ministry problems, career challenges? Why haven't you tapped into the power of the Holy Ghost to help you through these situations?

_____

_____

_____

5. Ezekiel saw dry bones come to life with a word from God. How important is the Word of God in your daily life? Are there words He is speaking to you through His Word the Bible that gives you the power to conquer any and every problem?

_____

_____

_____

_____

Meditation

"The Word came from the four corners of the earth. That tells me that there isn't an area that God cannot fill with the Holy Ghost—your past, your childhood, your feelings of inferiority, your wounds, your loneliness. The Holy Ghost can fill you from the north, south, east, and west."

Do you believe that within you is an army? No matter what others say, God sees incredible potential in you. You merely need to dispel satan's fear and allow the wind to breathe upon that which God has formed in you. Say a prayer now that it be so.

DAY 11

PENTECOST HAS
FULLY COME

And when the day of Pentecost was fully come, they were all with one accord in one place. And suddenly there cam a sound from Heaven as of a rushing mighty wind, and it filled all the house where they were sitting. And there appeared unto them cloven tongues like as of fire, and it sat upon each of them. And they were all filled with the Holy Ghost, and began to speak with other tongues, as the Spirit gave them utterance (Acts 2:1-4).

Excerpt: *Release Your Anointing*, Chapter 3.

The Jews were familiar with the term Pentecost. Everything God did in types and shadows in the Old Testament was fulfilled in the New Testament. In the Old Testament God revealed Himself in many ways to Israel. He was known as the "I Am," promising to sustain them on their journey from Egypt to Canaan.

Pentecost was a type of something that one day would explode and change this world for eternity. Everything that needed to precede Pentecost had taken place. Jesus, the Passover Lamb, had died and risen from the dead. He had walked with His disciples, was confirmed 40 days and nights with many infallible proofs, and then was received into glory.

Our personal Passover must precede our Pentecost. The blood of Christ prepares us for Pentecost, washing away our sin and prejudice, enabling us to come together with devout men and women from every nation.

Your Thoughts

1. Jesus was the *true* bread from Heaven (John 6:32). Do we receive Jesus as food from Heaven? Do we realize that God gave us Jesus to sustain our lives physically, mentally, emotionally, and spiritually? How do you acknowledge this ultimate gift?

_____

_____

_____

_____

_____

2. Have you allowed the blood of Christ to prepare you for Pentecost? Have your sins and prejudice been washed away?

_____

_____

_____

3. Are you guilty of devising a grading scale to judge the severity of certain sins of others? How about your own sins?

_____

_____

_____

4. God is tearing down racial, ethnic, and religious barriers to reach the entire world for Christ. Are you doing the same within your realm of influence?

_____

_____

_____

5. How can you better prepare yourself for your person-
    al Passover that precedes your Pentecost experience?

_____

_____

_____

_____

_____

_____

Meditation

"Pentecost marked the beginning of a mission for the Jews as
they gathered in the fruit of their labors. Pentecost in Act chapter
2 marks the beginning of a mission for the church to gather in lost
souls. We need Pentecost to fully arise in our lives as we fall in love
with Jesus, the Passover Lamb, to carry out the ingathering of His
harvest."

Have you experienced a personal Pentecost experience? In
what ways has it changed your perspective of life? Are you will to
share that experience with others?

DAY 12

WHY TONGUES?

In the law it is written, With men of other tongues and other lips will I speak unto this people; and yet for all that will they not hear Me, saith the Lord. Wherefore tongues are for a sign, not to them that believe, but to them that believe not: but prophesying serveth not for them that believe not, but for them which believe (1 Corinthians 14:21-22).

Excerpt: *Release Your Anointing*, Chapter 3.

God chose tongues as a sign of the Holy Spirit for a significant reason. He took the most difficult, uncontrollable member of our body and caused it to yield to divinely inspired speech. Bridling the tongue may be impossible for us to do in our own strength, but the supernatural outpouring of the Holy Ghost enabled the disciples to use their tongues for the purposes of God—and it will do the same for us.

Speaking in tongues can occur in two different settings. A believer may pray in tongues privately to commune with God (1 Cor. 14:2,4).

Scripture also teaches on the gift of tongues or "divers [different] kinds of tongues" (I Cor. 12:10), which is used in a public assembly.

When the gift of tongues is given in a public assembly, the message needs to be interpreted for the hearers to benefit (I Cor. 14:27). Sometimes, as on the day of Pentecost, the gift of tongues is given to minister to the hearers in their own language (Acts 2:6).

Isn't it amazing that men can hear the manifestation of the Holy Ghost but fail to believe? Mockers concluded, "These men are full of new wine" (Acts 2:13).

Your Thoughts

1. How easy is it for you to control your tongue? Do you find it to be, as James 3:2-8 says, something that is "untamable"?

   _____

   _____

2. Have you experienced praying in tongues privately to commune with God? What use does this ability have in the life of a believer?

   _____

   _____

3. Have you or someone you know received the gift of tongues for public assemblies? Why does this gift need to be accompanied by an interpretation of the tongue?

_____

_____

_____

_____

4. If you had been in the crowd on the Day of Pentecost after Jesus' ascension, what would you have thought if you had heard your native tongue being spoken by an unlearned fisherman? Why do you think the people responded by thinking the disciples were drunk?

_____

_____

_____

_____

5. Since the ability to pray in tongues is a sign of receiving the Holy Spirit, why do you think it is important that we all speak in tongues, as Paul says in First Corinthians 14:5? We should not look at this legalistically, but why should this experience be greatly encouraged for all believers?

_____

_____

_____

_____

Meditation

"When we are filled with the Holy Ghost, He acts as a deterrent. He places a bit in our mouths and bridles our speech. Just when you feel like telling someone off, the Holy Ghost takes control. Isn't it exciting that God took the tongue, a member of our body known for being "a fire, a world of iniquity," and sanctified it for His purposes?"

Have you experienced the Holy Spirit's power to bridle your tongue when you were about to say something that was not godly? How can we increase our ability to have the Holy Spirit control out tongue throughout our daily lives?

DAY 13

THE REFINER'S FIRE

I indeed baptize you with water unto repentance: but He that cometh after me is mightier than I, whose shoes I am not worthy to bear: He shall baptize you with the Holy Ghost, and with fire: Whose fan is in His hand, and He will thoroughly purge His floor, and gather His wheat into the garner; but He will burn up the chaff with unquenchable fire (Matthew 3:11-12).

Excerpt: *Release Your Anointing*, Chapter 3.

Fire will not destroy gold, but fire purifies gold. When God polishes His gold, He uses fiery trials. Unfortunately, nothing brings luster to your character and commitment to your heart like opposition does. The finished product is a result of the fiery process. Whenever you see someone shining with the kind of brilliancy that enables God to look down and see Himself, you are looking at someone who has been through the furnace of affliction.

Let me warn you: God places His prize possessions in the fire. The bad news is, even those who live godly lives will suffer persecution. The good news is, you might be in the fire, but God controls the thermostat! He knows how hot it needs to be to accomplish His purpose in your life.

His hand has fanned the flames that were needed to teach patience, prayer, and many other invaluable lessons. We don't enjoy them, but we need them. What a joy to know that He cares enough to straighten out the jagged places in our lives. It is His fatherly corrections that confirm us as legitimate children—not illegitimate ones. He affirms my position in Him by correcting and chastening me.

Your Thoughts

I. If you are God's investment of gold, does it stand to reason that He would want to have the purest gold possible? How does His desire for purity within us benefit us?

_____

_____

_____

_____

_____

_____

2. Have you ever been through a fiery process that you knew was God's refining fire in your life? If so, how did this process work to take out the impurities in your character?

_____

_____

_____

_____

3. Name someone who shines as brilliant pure gold, reflecting the Father. What characteristics do they have that make them seem so pure to you? What kinds of trials might they have gone through to receive that purity?

_____

_____

_____

_____

4. Knowing that God has control of the thermostat during our purification can give us comfort. Why? How does trusting Him during the process of refinement help us see past the immediate pain?

_____

_____

_____

_____

_____

5. What are some areas of your life that God is purifying right now? How does His Fatherhood come to bear when He places you in the fire? Why do we need this process?

_____

_____

_____

_____

_____

Meditation

"It is impossible to discuss the value of investing in people and not find ourselves worshiping God—what a perfect picture of investment. God is the major stockholder.... The greatest primary investment He made was the inflated, unthinkable price of redemption that He paid. What He did on the Cross was worship. Normally the lesser worships the greater, but this time, the greater worshiped the lesser. What an investment!"

How has God made an investment in you? How have you made an investment in others? Do you think God sees your investment in other people as an act of worship?

DAY 14

HIS INVESTMENT

Verily, verily, I say unto you, Except a corn of wheat fall into the ground and die, it abideth alone: but if it die, it bringeth forth much fruit (John 12:24).

Excerpt: *Release Your Anointing*, Chapter 3.

God has an investment in our lives. First of all, no one invests without the expectation of gain. The apostle Paul wrote, "But we have this treasure in earthen vessels, that the excellency of the power may be of God, and not of us," (2 Cor. 4:7). Thus, according to Scripture, we possess treasure. However, the excellency of what we have is not of us, but of God. The treasure is *of* God. It is accumulated in us and then presented back to Him.

We are fertile ground—broken by troubles, enriched by failures, and watered with tears. Yet undeniably there is a deposit within us. This deposit is valuable enough to place us on satan's hit list. Paul prayed that "the eyes of your understanding being enlightened…" (Eph. 1:18). Paul challenged them to become progressively aware of the enormity of His inheritance in us, not our

inheritance in Him. We spend most of our time talking about what we want from God. The real issue is what He wants from us. It is the Lord who has the greatest investment. We are the parched, dry ground from which Christ springs. Believe me, God is serious about His investment!

Your Thoughts

1. If no one invests without the expectation of gain, how would God Almighty, who has all resources, decide to invest for His gain? What gain do you think God sees in us to prove His investment in us is wise?

_____

_____

_____

2. What treasure has God placed inside you? What spiritual fruit has been seen by others within your life? What gifts have you employed? What kind of positive character traits have you used for God's glory?

_____

_____

_____

3. What makes a person have *fertile ground*? What has produced fertile ground in your life? Do you think you are ready and fertile for God's investment today?

_____

_____

_____

_____

4. The deposit God has made places us on satan's hit list. Have you sensed this threat at any time in your life? Why does satan dislike the deposit within us? What is his strategy for stopping God's investment from maturing to great gain?

_____

_____

_____

_____

5. Why should we be talking more about what *God* wants from us than what *we* want from God? In your opinion, how does God view His inheritance in you?

_____

_____

_____

_____

_____

Meditation

"It has been suggested that if you walk in the Spirit, you won't have to contend with the fire. Real faith doesn't mean you won't go through the fire, however. Real faith simply means that when you pass through the fire, He will be with you. This thought brings you to an unusual reality.... The presence of the Lord can turn a burning inferno into a walk in the park!"

Have you ever felt disillusionment because you thought you could escape trials once you became a Christian? How have real trials helped you sense God's presence? Are there current trials that have revealed to you your need to sense God's presence?

DAY 15

FAITH

Quenched the violence of fire, escaped the edge of the sword, out of weakness were made strong, waxed valiant in fight, turned to flight the armies of the aliens (Hebrews 11:34).

Excerpt: *Release Your Anointing*, Chapter 3.

Hebrews chapter 11 discusses at length the definition of faith. It then shares the deeds of faith in verses 32-35a, and finally it discusses the perseverance of faith in verses 35b-39. There are distinctions of faith as well. In Hebrews 11:32-35a, the teaching has placed an intensified kind of emphasis on the distinct faith that escapes peril and overcomes obstacles.

However, in the verses that end the chapter, the writer deals with the distinctions of another kind of faith. In his closing remarks, he shares that there were some other believers whose faith was exemplified *through* suffering and not *from* suffering (Heb. 11:36-37).

Christianity's foundation is not built on elite mansions, stocks, and bonds, or sports cars and cruise-control living. The Church is built on the backs of men and women who withstood discomfort for a cause. These people were not the end but the means where-by God was glorified. Some of them exhibited their faith through their shadows' healing sick people. Still others exhibited their faith by bleeding to death beneath piles of stone. They also had a brand of faith that seemed to ease the effect, though it didn't alter the cause.

Your Thoughts

1. Define faith in your own words. How does your definition compare or contrast with the one given in Hebrews chapter 11?

   _____

   _____

   _____

2. What is the difference between deeds that are done by us as we strive in our power and will versus those that are done by faith? Do you have examples of these from your own life?

   _____

   _____

   _____

3. How do you think someone "perseveres" in faith? How does perseverance help grow our faith? What makes our faith distinct so we can escape peril and overcome obstacles?

_____

_____

_____

_____

_____

4. How is faith exemplified *through* suffering? How does this type of faith encourage other believers? How does it bring a witness to the world?

_____

_____

_____

_____

5. What do you think the following means: "These people were not the end but the means whereby God was glorified"? Are you an example of faith to those around you? Does your faith bring glory to God?

_____

_____

_____

_____

_____

Meditation

"As the fire of persecution forces us to make deeper levels of commitment, it is so important that our faith be renewed to match our level of commitment. There is a place in God where the fire consumes every other desire but to know the Lord in the power of His resurrection. At this level all other pursuits tarnish and seem worthless in comparison."

How do you renew your faith? What process do you go through? How can you be prepared to face persecution through your growth in faith?

DAY 16

SECRET CODE

Surely the Lord God will do nothing, but He revealeth His secret unto his servants the prophets (Amos 3:7).

Excerpt: *Release Your Anointing*, Chapter 4.

God has spoken to His people from the very beginning (Gen. 3:8). God spoke to His people through the prophets (Heb. 1:1). He also spoke to us by His Son (Heb.1:2). He spoke to us by miracles (Heb.2:4). He then spoke by His apostles. As a result of the mighty outpouring at Pentecost, God said He would speak through His Spirit (Joel 2:28).

God is speaking a vital message in these last days. He is looking for someone to deliver a timely, life-changing word. Many times, however, it is in secret code and can only be understood by those who have the Holy Ghost.

When God speaks in secret, He does so for at least two reasons:

1. God wants to have an intimate relationship with you. You tell your secrets and innermost thoughts only to your closest, most trusted friends.

2. By speaking in secret code, God insures that the devil does not understand the strategy of the church. This enables us to make an unannounced surprise attack because the secret code bypasses the radar and defense system of the satanic forces in opposition to us (Eph. 6:12).

Your Thoughts

1. Think through the ways God has revealed Himself in the Old Testament. To whom did He speak face to face? Do you know examples of Old Testament people who heard God speak? What were some of the situations when this communication took place?

_____

_____

_____

_____

_____

_____

2. How do we know that Jesus spoke only the Words of the Father? Why do you think people so easily received His words? Why were there so many who did not receive?

_____

_____

_____

3. What are some examples of when God spoke through the apostles? Highlight things you remember He told us through them.

_____

_____

_____

4. How can you be sure that God really wants to speak important messages to us today? What do you think you need to do to be in the receiving position to hear Him?

_____

_____

5. As God speaks in secret code, why doesn't satan understand what He says? How does it make you feel to understand that God speaks with His most trusted friends?

_____

_____

_____

_____

Meditation

"Many try to limit God, saying He has spoken in the past but has ceased to speak today. This, however, is not true....

"The Holy Ghost also speaks to us today. Tongues are God's message for the last days. It isn't the only way that He can speak, but it is one avenue of speech. We need faith to allow Him to speak and interpret the message through a willing vessel."

We may believe that others have limited God because they do not believe in the gifts He still gives to us today. But first we may need to look at the log in our own eyes. Take time before the Lord and ask Him to reveal to you if there have been times when you lacked the faith to allow Him to speak to you more intimately.

DAY 17

MYSTERIES OF THE KINGDOM

If ye love Me, keep My commandments. And I will pray the Father, and He shall give you another Comforter, that He may abide with you for ever; Even the Spirit of truth; whom the world cannot receive, because it seeth Him not, neither knoweth Him: but ye know Him; for He dwelleth with you, and shall be in you (John 14:15-17).

Excerpt: *Release Your Anointing,* Chapter 4.

This Scripture indicates the Kingdom of God was going through some drastic changes.

1. We find the changing of the guard. "I will pray the Father, and he shall give you another Comforter" (vs. 16).

2. We find an obligation on our part to receive the Holy Ghost. Jesus said, "If Ye love me, keep My commandments" (vs. 15). As a result of our obedience, Jesus said that He would pray to the Father. He in turn would send another Comforter to us.

3. Jesus said three things about the Holy Ghost in John 14:17:

- The world cannot receive Him.

- The world cannot see Him, because His ways are not their ways; He is a mystery to them.

- The world doesn't know Him.

All the miracles of Christ declared what His followers would do in that day. Because the world did not receive Him, did not see Him, and did not know Him, they crucified the Lord of glory.

God calls those who are committed to excellence to a place of seclusion and aloneness. The Holy Ghost is saying, "Detach yourself from things that blind you from seeing My mysteries and deafen you from hearing My language."

Your Thoughts

1. In your own words, summarize the ways that John 14:15-17 shows that the Kingdom of God was going through some drastic changes. How were these changes important to what would happen following Christ's ascension?

_____

_____

_____

2. Why are we "obliged" to receive the Holy Ghost?
    Why is this obligation more than a mere choice? If
    Jesus said He would pray for us to receive the Holy
    Ghost, how should we pray?

    _____

    _____

    _____

3. How does receiving the Holy Ghost separate us from
    the world? In what ways is this an opportunity for
    the world to look to us, the Church, as a source of
    healing for them?

    _____

    _____

4. How do the miracles that Jesus performed show us
    what we are to do? Think through some of those
    miracles and list some. Are these part of our current
    job description?

    _____

    _____

5. How does seclusion and aloneness bring us to a place of excellence? How do times of retreat help blind our eyes to the world and open our ears to the Holy Ghost?

_____

_____

_____

_____

Meditation

"Jesus is speaking, but even those in the Church are missing Him because they do not hear His language. Many are not hearing His voice because tradition has left them content with only the first glimpse of His glory. The glory of Christ far exceeds any glory ever known by man. In those three short years Jesus began to reveal the mysteries of a powerful Kingdom that was greater than any problem, sickness, or dilemma."

In what ways do you think the Church is missing what Jesus is speaking? What mysteries does He desire to share with the Church that will help His Kingdom in these last days? Are you available to hear these mysteries? Why or why not?

DAY 18

LIGHT AND SALT

You are the salt of the earth: but if the salt has lost his savour, wherewith shall it be salted? It is thenceforth good for nothing, but to be cast out, and to be trodden under foot of men (Matthew 5:13).

Excerpt: *Release Your Anointing*, Chapter 4.

As the Church allows the Holy Ghost to work in and through us, the world will begin to see Jesus and the Kingdom of God in action. It will be a mystery to the world but a powerful reality to the Church. But it won't happen overnight. It's progressive, day by day, trial by trial, storm by storm, valley by valley, and temptation by temptation.

When Jesus was on earth, He said, "I am the light of the world: he that followeth Me shall not walk in darkness, but shall have the light of life" (John 8:12).

But when He died, darkness covered the earth. Except for the Holy Ghost, darkness will prevail.

We are beacons, lighthouses to a world of storm-tossed, beaten, battered individuals. We are to be a city set on a hill and illuminated by the Holy Ghost. Our joy, peace, righteousness should shine brightly, encouraging others to find refuge in our God. The fruit of the Spirit in our lives acts as a magnet to draw them to Jesus.

Salt does several things: creates thirst, preserves, burns wounds, and seasons.

Your Thoughts

1. Are you a lighthouse in a dark world? Is your light flickering in the window or shining brightly from the rooftop?

    _____

    _____

    _____

2. Are you seasoning those around you with the taste of God's grace and mercy? If not, what are some ways in which you can spread His seasoning to friends and family?

    _____

    _____

    _____

3. Are your joy, peace, and righteousness shining for all to see? Do you think it is important for Christians to be a beacon of light to others—even if they don't "feel" like it?

_____

_____

_____

_____

4. Have you given the Holy Ghost permission to saturate your very being with His salt and light so you can then pass it on to sad and desperate people around you?

_____

_____

_____

_____

5. Allowing God to use you as salt and light fulfills your God-given destiny.

_____

_____

_____

_____

_____

_____

Meditation

"When Jesus walked the earth, He was a preservative for the world. A thief could not die without first being preserved by His forgiveness (Luke 23:42); a widow's only son, the apple of her eye, could not reach the gates of death with Jesus stopping the funeral procession (Luke 7:12). Lazarus could not lay decomposing in a tomb without hearing a voice, 'Lazarus, come forth!' (John 11:43)."

Are you preserving, stopping, calling, shining?

DAY 19

GOD HAS YOUR NUMBER

The people that do know their God shall be strong, and do exploits
(Daniel 11:32).

Excerpt: *Release Your Anointing*, Chapter 4.

God is ringing your telephone today. He may have to call you to give you a message for someone else, who for one reason or another, cannot hear. The only way the message can get through is for you to speak out what God has spoken into your spirit. Be sure to pray for an interpreter.

Many anointed people wrongly believe that their anointing gives them the right to get out of order. They may exercise their gift, but the message of God is misrepresented, wrong, or even damaging. This confuses and wounds people.

And the spirits of the prophets are subject to the prophets
(1 Corinthians 14:32).

Timeliness is an important issue with the gift of tongues. Your anointing may not always be in dispute as much as your timing. If your message is not given in its proper timing, it can hurt, confuse, and mislead. The Holy Spirit is not unseemly. He does not cause disorder.

God is looking for a Church who believes He can confirm them and their ministry with gifts, signs and wonders in the Holy Ghost. (See Hebrews 2:3-4 and Mark 16:17-18.)

Your Thoughts

1. Have you ever experienced receiving a message that was not for you only? How does God work in this way? Why does He do so?

   _____

   _____

2. In what ways can people justify being out of order because they have received a message from God for others? When we get a message for others, we have a responsibility not only to deliver it in purity, but to deliver it when God asks us to do so. Why?

   _____

   _____

   _____

3. What does submission have to do with the public
    use of any gift? Who are we to be submitted to in
    Heaven and on earth? Why?

    _____

    _____

    _____

    _____

4. How can the mistake of not being timely with your gifts
    work against your anointing? When someone in authori-
    ty does not receive your gift, what should you do?

    _____

    _____

    _____

    _____

    _____

5. If God wants to entrust us with His ministry gifts,
    how can we prepare ourselves to learn timeliness and
    submission before we "train wreck" the expression of
    those gifts? If our hearts are right, what else needs to
    be right so we do not hurt, confuse, or mislead others?

    _____

    _____

    _____

    _____

Meditation

"Don't be dismayed if those who see you say, 'These people
are fanatics!' The Holy Ghost will cause a division between truth
and falsehood. When you begin to function in the gift of God for
your life and the devil sees a true manifestation of the Holy
Ghost, expect to be put on the devil's hit list. This is nothing more
than a trick of the enemy to get you to stop."

Honestly think through your feelings if other people thought
you were a fanatic because you spoke in tongues. Why would such
a division be expected? What do you need to do to prepare your
emotions and your spirit if you are rejected because of your
beliefs?

DAY 20

MESSAGES FROM HEAVEN

Eye hath not seen, nor ear heard, neither have entered into the heart of man, the things which God hath prepared for them that love him. But God hath revealed them unto us by his Spirit: for the Spirit searcheth all things, yea, the deep things of God (I Corinthians 2:9-10).

Excerpt: *Release Your Anointing*, Chapter 4.

L et's look at seven areas of your life in which the Holy Ghost wants to speak.

1. The Holy Ghost wants to speak to you things that go beyond human logic, natural tendency, and physical comprehension (I Cor. 2:9-10).

2. The Holy Ghost will testify to you (Rom. 8:16).

3. The Holy Ghost will give you direction (Acts 8:29). Sometimes the message for yourself, others give direction.

4. The Holy Ghost speaks to lead us to obedience (Acts 10:1-23).

5. The Holy Ghost shows you God's choice for companionship (Acts 13:2).

6. The Holy Ghost will speak and close doors that were the right thing but the wrong time (Acts 16:6-7).

7. The Holy Ghost sometimes warns us (Acts 21:4).

The Holy Ghost speaks for a variety of reasons. His word may be for you or someone else. He may testify to your spirit of God's faithfulness.

Instead of questions for Your Thoughts,
think through the seven areas and fill out the following chart.

AREA	SCRIPTURAL EXAMPLE Who, what, where, when, how, why	PERSONAL EXAMPLE
1.		
2.		
3.		
4.		
5.		
6.		
7.		

Meditation

"God is trying to intervene in your life. He may use you to intervene in the life of someone who may not be answering His call. Whatever the case, you can be confident that it is right because our *parakletos*, the Holy Ghost, speaks only the counsel He has heard in Heaven."

How do you think God is trying to intervene in your life? Why is your confidence important to be able to use the gifts that God has given to you? How does it make you feel to know that you can receive the counsel of Heaven?

DAY 21

THE TRANSFORMER

But as many as received Him, to them gave He power to become the sons of God, even to them that believe on His name (John 1:12).

Excerpt: *Release Your Anointing*, Chapter 5.

I pray that we as Christians never lose our conviction that God does change lives. We must protect this message. Our God enables us to make the radical changes necessary for fulfilling our purposes and responsibilities. Like the caterpillar that eats and sleeps its way into change, the process occurs gradually, but nonetheless powerfully. Many people who will rock this world are sleeping in the cocoon of obscurity, waiting for their change to come. The Scriptures declare, "...it is high time to awake out of sleep: for now is our salvation nearer than when we believed" (Rom. 13:11).

God made the *first* transformer! He created man from dust. He created him in such a way that, if need be, He could pull a woman out of him without ever having to reach back into the dust. Out of one creative act God transformed the man into a marriage. Then He transformed the marriage into a family, the family into a society. God never had to reach into the ground again because the power to transform was intrinsically placed into man. All types of potential were locked into our spirits before birth.

For the Christian, transformation at its optimum is the outworking of the internal. God placed certain things in us that must come out. We house the prophetic power of God. Every word of our personal prophetic destiny is inside us. He has ordained us to be!

Your Thoughts

1. How strong is your conviction that God does change lives? Have you seen evidence of this among the people in your spiritual family? Why is this conviction important to our ability to change?

_____

_____

_____

2. What do you think God is doing as people remain in obscurity waiting for their time to rock the world? How does progressive change work in your life?

_____

_____

3. God's business of transformation began with Adam. Think through all the possibilities God placed in Adam—what are some of these possibilities? What possibilities do you think God placed within you?

_____

_____

_____

_____

4. Why does God put potential within our spirits before we are born? What does this potential have to do with our destiny in God's Kingdom?

_____

_____

_____

_____

5. How does God make us aware of our potential? How does He give us experience and training to bring this potential to external fruition?

_____

_____

_____

_____

_____

Meditation

"You are empowered by God to reach and accomplish goals that transcend human limitations! It is important that every vessel God uses realize that he or she was able to accomplish what others could not only because God gave them the grace to do so. God works out the internal destinies of His children. He gives us the power to become who we are eternally and internally."

Have you felt empowered by God to accomplish more than you could on your own? How has God's grace worked in your life? Meditate on the ways He has given you power to become who you are eternally and internally.

DAY 22

ORCHESTRATING CHANGE

And be not conformed to this world: but be ye transformed by the renewing of your mind, that ye may prove what is that good, and acceptable, and perfect, will of God (Romans 12:2).

Excerpt: *Release Your Anointing,* Chapter 5.

It would be a sad day for the unsaved if the Holy Spirit stopped convicting people and drawing them to the Savior. Let's look at His work in the world today:

According to the passage in Romans, the Holy Ghost has arrested you on three counts:

1. He has reproved your sin, which means to convict, to expose, to convince of a wrong, to tell a fault.

2. He convinces you of righteousness or a right standing with God. His goodness, not your own, saves you.

3. He will convince you of judgment, not only of your future encounter with God, but also of ungodly influences that cause you to sin.

The Holy Ghost wants to orchestrate change in your life. Because you have messed up, many of you believe your calling has been annulled. The devil is a liar, for "the gifts and callings of God are without repentance" (Rom. 11:29).

The Holy Ghost has come to convince and influence you to change. Dare to be different! Refuse to become a part of the mundane crowd going nowhere. Rise up and shake yourself. Find yourself a church that is reflecting change by the influence of the Holy Ghost.

Your Thoughts

1. How did the Holy Spirit draw you to the Savior? Is He currently working on any people within your sphere of relationships?

   _____

   _____

   _____

   _____

   _____

2. How has the Holy Ghost convicted you of sin? Have you ever been embarrassed when your sin was exposed? How has the Holy Spirit convinced you that you were wrong when you thought you were right?

_____

_____

_____

3. What did you think when the Holy Spirit convinced you that without Jesus you would not be able to stand before God? How did He present righteousness to you so you could understand God's grace through Jesus?

_____

_____

4. How has the Holy Ghost convinced you that God's judgment is real? What are some of the ungodly influences that will bring sin to your life?

_____

_____

5. Why do you think God does not annul our callings when we have sinned so greatly? How hard is it to believe that you can change from whatever you have been to what God wants you to be?

_____

_____

_____

_____

Meditation

"Change is a gift from God.... The Bible calls change *repentance*. Repentance is God's gift to a struggling heart who wants to find himself. Without the Holy Spirit's help you can search and search and still not find repentance. One moment with the Spirit of God can lead you into a place of renewal that, on your own, you would not find or enjoy."

Why do you think it is difficult for most of us to process change? If repentance is at the root of change, do you think it becomes even more difficult? Why or why not? Ask the Lord to help you embrace change and repentance as much as you embrace blessing.

DAY 23

THE HOLY SPIRIT'S
INFLUENCE ·

Nevertheless I tell you the truth; It is expedient for you that I go away: for if I go not away, the Comforter will not come to you; but if I depart, I will send Him unto you (John 16:7).

Excerpt: *Release Your Anointing,* Chapter 5.

The Holy Spirit brings His influence in the following five areas:

1. The Holy Ghost sets the stage for the Word of God (Gen. 1:2).

The Spirit did the preparatory work for the Word to give the command: "Let there be…."

2. The Holy Spirit's influence will separate and declare (Gen. 1:4-8).

The Holy Spirit will separate certain things from you, set limitations, and declare your destiny.

3. The Holy Spirit wants to resurrect buried seeds in your life (Gen. 1:11-12). The seeds were there, but they were obscured.

God formed man from dust. But man is merely a form of what he can be before the Holy Spirit breathes into him vibrancy and freshness of life.

4. The Holy Spirit wrestles with us to bring us to a deeper commitment.

We need the Holy Spirit to go before us, preparing people's hearts and minds for the Word. If the Holy Ghost truly comes upon you, He will change your life.

5. The Holy Spirit seeks a place to rest in authority (Gen. 8:8-12).

As Jesus stood in the Jordan, the dove descended from Heaven, landed on Him, and His authority and anointing rested on Jesus.

Your Thoughts

1. In what ways has the Holy Ghost set the stage for God's Word in your life? Have you allowed the Holy Ghost to continuously prepare you to receive more of God's Word?

_____

_____

2. How has the Holy Spirit separated and declared things to you so you were clear on right and wrong, good and better? Have you experienced any limitations from the Holy Spirit? Has He declared your destiny?

_____

_____

_____

_____

3. Before you were a Christian you were like Adam, just a form of a person. How did the Holy Spirit breathe life into you so you could receive the salvation that comes from Jesus Christ? How did the seeds that were planted in you before you were born then come to life?

_____

_____

_____

_____

4. Have you ever felt as if you were wrestling with the Holy Spirit? Have you felt God pulling or tugging you forward but the boundaries of your comfort zone held you back? How does the Holy Ghost change us so we can grow into a deeper commitment with God?

    _____

    _____

    _____

    _____

5. What authority has the Holy Spirit rested upon your shoulders? When you receive divine authority, how can the Holy Spirit give the fullness needed to accomplish the responsibilities of that authority?

    _____

    _____

    _____

    _____

Meditation

"The Holy Spirit wants to resurrect buried seeds in your life (see Gen. 1:11-12). The seeds were there, but they were obscured. God brought forth creatures from the waters (see Gen. 1:20). They were there, but the Word brought them forth from what had covered them. God commanded the earth to bring forth living creatures (see Gen. 1:24). They were there, but simply had to be brought forth."

How excited would you be if you suddenly inherited a stash of gold or priceless jewels from a distant relative? Do you think this same excitement could be yours as the Spirit moves and the Word reveals your God-given destiny? Would there be excitement in Heaven as well?

DAY 24

GOD MINES FOR GOLD

But He knoweth the way that I take; when He hath tried me, I shall come forth as gold (Job 23:10).

Excerpt: *Release Your Anointing,* Chapter 5.

Job endured tremendous emotional pain and physical affliction. His troubles were not only known to God but were allowed by God. Losing his sons and daughters and possessions left Job feeling very much alone.

Every gold mine is hidden beneath the earth. Mining priceless jewels takes years of painstaking labor. Tons of earth must be removed.

In the same way, a gold mine is buried beneath your flesh. Crucifying your flesh is excruciating, but it must occur to reveal the gifts within you. Give God digging rights. After all, the mine belongs to Him.

Your Thoughts

1. How deep are your jewels hidden? Will it take years
    to uncover them, or will you allow the Holy Ghost
    to blow away the earth with His breath of life?

    _____

    _____

    _____

    _____

2. Have you given God the digging rights to your gold
    mine? Take an active step right now to sign over all
    rights to Him.

    _____

    _____

    _____

    _____

3. What jewels and gifts do you think are waiting to be discovered within you? Have you purposely allowed them to lay dormant? Why?

_____

_____

_____

_____

4. While you are hoping to expose your jewels and gifts, satan is hoping to keep them hidden. Do you ever feel weary from the battle?

_____

_____

_____

_____

_____

5. How can prayer ease the fatigue and lessen the hurt from battle scars?

_____

_____

_____

_____

_____

_____

Meditation

"The devil knows you're a gold mine waiting to be claimed and mined. Your adversary has covered your priceless jewels with your past, unconfessed sins, emotional traumas, and religious tradition. Little does the devil know that you have been buried alive. You merely need the Spirit to move, and the Word uncovers you. You are Heaven's best kept secret and hell's worst nightmare."

Allowing the Holy Spirit to move within us will defeat satan and foil his attempts to keep our jewels hidden. Pray for the Spirit to move mightily.

DAY 25

WHEN WINNING IS LOSING

Therefore leaving the principles of the doctrine of Christ, let us go on unto perfection; not laying again the foundation of repentance from dead works, and of faith toward God, Of the doctrine of baptisms, and of laying on of hands, and of resurrection of the dead, and of eternal judgment. And this will we do, if God permit (Hebrews 6:1-3).

Excerpt: *Release Your Anointing*, Chapter 5.

As the Holy Spirit strives with you to bring you into submission and obedience, you may be holding on to the very thing that He wants. As you walk away you may feel as though you've won, but you've actually lost.

Some of you have matured, and the Holy Spirit wants to take you higher. But it's a choice. God asks you to push away from the familiar into the supernatural. People resist change, but in order to get to where God wants us—and to arrive on time—you must push away.

The Holy Spirit flew on missions in the Old Testament as He rested on Abraham, Isaac, and Jacob, but they were not the one.

Finally, He looked from the portals of glory and saw the One. There was only One found worthy in Heaven and earth for the dove to land upon—Jesus.

When Jesus was dying, He said, "Father, into thy hands I commend [put into your trust] my spirit" (Luke 23:46). This same dove swept down from glory as a mighty rushing wind (Acts 2:2). He found a body, the Church, to inhabit and to rest His authority upon.

Your Thoughts

1. How does the Holy Spirit bring you to submission and obedience? What methods does He use to get your attention and convince you to make a change?

_____

_____

_____

_____

_____

_____

2. Rate your maturity over the last five years. Has the Holy Spirit taken you on a steady progression of growth? Have there been peaks and valleys in the continuum of your maturing?

_____

_____

3. Why do we have to push away from something in order to receive change and get to where God wants us? Does this show how our will is involved in change? What does timing have to do with change?

_____

_____

4. Review how the Holy Spirit worked in the lives of Old Testament heroes and New Testament apostles. What are some of the miracles they performed that seem completely out of their reach? How did the Holy Spirit work within them to change them?

_____

_____

5. As a member of the Church, you have been given the same Spirit that lived in Jesus. What does this awareness mean to you? Whose authority do you have?

_____

_____

_____

_____

_____

Meditation

"We can attain a place in God that is higher than our problems, giving us a divine perspective. We must be led to this place. It is against our nature to want this rock. We must oppose our flesh and say, 'When my spirit is overwhelmed, my spirit goes beyond nature and finds satisfaction only in the supernatural.' We ask God to lead us to the rock—Jesus—and away from earthly logic."

Have you ever experienced a mountaintop perspective on a situation or challenge? As you looked down from God's perspective, how did He change your attitude? How did He adjust your logic?

DAY 26

DO YOU WANT CHILDREN?

The Holy Ghost shall come upon thee, and the power of the Highest shall overshadow thee: therefore also that holy thing which shall be born of thee shall be called the Son of God (Luke 1:35).

Excerpt: *Release Your Anointing*, Chapter 6.

Many Christians never conceive a child. Many do not want children because they do not want commitment and responsibility. Many have been impregnated by the Holy Ghost but have chosen to abort the baby. Other Christians who cannot carry their baby to term have miscarried.

The womb was designed as a receptacle for the seed of man and a place for a conceived child to develop. The Bible says Adam knew his wife (see Gen. 4:1,25). This intimate relationship gave them a son. You can trace the lineage of Christ back to the fruit of this first intimate relationship.

Mary was a virgin when the angel announced she would have a baby. She asked, "How shall this be, seeing I know not a man?" (Luke 1:34). This child was conceived by the power of the Holy Ghost.

Three things were to happen:

1. Conception—"Thou shalt conceive" (Luke 1:31).

2. Intimacy—"The Holy Ghost shall come upon thee."

3. Implanting of the Seed—"The power of the Highest shall overshadow thee."

It was totally the work of the Holy Ghost, but He had to have a womb in which to do His work.

Your Thoughts

1. Why is it so important that our intimacy with the Holy Spirit bears children? Why aren't we just permitted to have a honeymoon relationship that lasts for eternity?

_____

_____

_____

_____

_____

2. When two people commit to the responsibility of biological children, what are the considerations they need to entertain? When we commit to the responsibility of spiritual children, what are the considerations we need to entertain?

_____

_____

_____

3. What do you think it means to conceive spiritual children? What process might this take?

_____

_____

4. What does "intimacy with the Holy Ghost" mean to you? Does it have to do with *quantity* of time? Does it have to do with *quality* of time?

_____

_____

_____

5. How does the "implanting of the seed" take place in terms of spiritual progeny? Why does the Holy Spirit have to be the One who does the implanting? What does it take for us to be ready for this event?

_____

_____

_____

_____

Meditation

"Many are afraid to fall in love with the Holy Ghost because they know that commitment brings intimacy, and intimacy brings conception, and conception brings labor, and labor produces a baby. As in the natural realm, it takes an intimate relationship to conceive.... [but] they do not want to endure nine months of carrying the child."

What do you think of the strings that are tied to a relationship with the Holy Ghost? Does this impose a stiff responsibility on you that you do not want to bear? What kind of a commitment do you need to make with the Holy Ghost to revitalize an intimate relationship with Him?

DAY 27

WHO ARE YOU INWARDLY?

The spirit of man is the candle of the Lord, searching all the inward parts of the belly (Proverbs 20:27).

Excerpt: *Release Your Anointing,* Chapter 6.

Man is made in God's image and likeness. We are also a triune being—body, soul, and spirit. God has saved our spirits. Our bodies are not saved. The body does not want to be holy or bring forth good fruit. Your body will never tell you to pray. The body will never encourage you to live right. The body will never restrain you from gossiping. The body is flesh and will always be flesh.

David prayed, "Search me, O God, and know my heart: try me, and know my thoughts" (Ps. 139:23).

What does God use to search us? Read Proverbs 20:27 again. This verse shows us three truths:

1. Man is not only body and soul, but also spirit.

2. The spirit of man is the candle of the Lord.

3. The Lord uses this spirit to search the innermost being of humans.

Underneath your shout, your dance, your speaking in tongues, who are you really? This has always been the problem with man-made holiness. Trying to change a person outwardly only leaves him or her frustrated, confused, and feeling like a failure.

God does just the opposite. He changes you from the inside out.

Your Thoughts

1. If you were to explain how you were created in God's image, what would you say? How are you made in His likeness?

_____

_____

_____

_____

_____

_____

2. What is the difference between the body and the soul? What do you think makes up the soul of a person? What is the difference between the soul and the spirit? How do all three of these make up who you are?

_____

_____

_____

3. What limitations does your body impose or try to impose on your soul? How does your body get in the way of your spirit? What must you do to overcome your body's limitations?

_____

_____

4. Is it unsettling to you to be like David and invite God to search you thoroughly? Why or why not? Why is it important for us to invite God to search us?

_____

_____

_____

5. What does Proverbs 20:27 speak to your heart about your spirit? How does your innermost part truly reflect who you are as opposed to the outward appearance you have?

_____

_____

_____

_____

Meditation

"Changing from the outside in has no lasting effect. It always leaves the womb barren, crying, 'It's not enough!' Changing from the outside in is like painting a building without removing the trash that clutters the inside.

There is a difference between repainting and *repenting*. *Repainting* changes the outside, repenting changes the inside."

Have you ever repainted a situation instead of repenting? The trouble with repainting is eventually the paint peels away leaving the original problem. Do you remember a problem that you thought was taken care of only to have it reemerge? Could have repenting rather than repainting solved the problem the first time?

DAY 28

OUR SPIRITS ARE JOINED

The Spirit itself beareth witness with our spirit, that we are the children of God (Romans 8:16).

Excerpt: *Release Your Anointing*, Chapter 6.

This Scripture deals with two spirits—the spirit of man and the Holy Spirit. Joined together at salvation, the Holy Spirit testifies to our spirit that we are saved. He can testify in your spirit when all hell is breaking loose.

Have you ever wanted something and knew it was God's will, but you just couldn't seem to get a breakthrough? As you see someone with the very thing you want, it causes a kicking inside you. This lets you know that your baby is still there. You haven't aborted or miscarried. The Holy Spirit lets you know it's still in you.

What happens next is simply awesome. The Holy Spirit becomes so much of a part of your life that you begin to have more than just a Sunday morning fling with Him. You begin to know the Holy Spirit and understand His purpose. You become sensitive to His feelings, which keep you from grieving the Holy Spirit. You begin to feel a burning love and appreciation for the

Holy Spirit, which helps you to obey and submit to His leading. This keeps the flame of spiritual passion burning in your spirit.

Your Thoughts

1. What is the difference between the spirit of a man and the Spirit of God? How do they work together within us?

    _____

    _____

    _____

    _____

2. How has the Holy Ghost worked inside you to testify to your salvation? How has He given you a witness during trials or challenges?

    _____

    _____

    _____

    _____

3. When we have a desire, how do we know that it is God's will for us? When we know the desire is God's will, how does the Holy Spirit give us a witness? How does this bring confidence to our souls?

    _____

    _____

    _____

    _____

4. Have you ever been so infatuated with someone that it was hard to concentrate because of the mini day-dreams you had about your relationship? In what way do you think we should be so in love with God, that the Holy Spirit overwhelms us in even a greater way?

    _____

    _____

    _____

    _____

5. As in a relationship with a close friend or spouse, we begin to "read their minds," how does regular, frequent intimacy with the Holy Ghost allow us to know the mind of God?

_____

_____

_____

_____

_____

Meditation

"As a result of your daily communion with the Holy Spirit, the barren areas in your life that have cried out for years—the spiritual womb that has never been satisfied—now becomes impregnated by the Holy Spirit.... We supply the womb; the Holy Ghost supplies the seed; our relationship with God brings about conception. As we bring forth spiritual offspring, they should resemble the Father."

Think through the process of an intimate relationship with the Holy Ghost. How has this process occurred in your life? What stage is your relationship in at present?

DAY 29

THERMOMETER OR
THERMOSTAT?

But the fruit of the Spirit is love, joy, peace, longsuffering, gentleness, goodness, faith, meekness, temperance: against such there is no law (Galatians 5:22-23).

Excerpt: *Release Your Anointing,* Chapter 6.

The Holy Ghost functions like a thermostat and a thermometer. The thermometer reflects its surrounding temperature, and the thermostat controls the inside heating system that gives the thermometer its reading.

In the same way, the Holy Ghost works inside you. Your outward actions reflect your temperature to those around you.

Galatians 5:22-23 describes three sets of triplets:

1. Atmosphere.

2. Attitude.

3. Attribute.

The atmosphere is your surroundings. The Holy Spirit will build a fire of His own that will bring warmth to a cold atmosphere. This is why the first three triplets—love, joy, and peace—are atmosphere-changing fruit.

The second three triplets—longsuffering, gentleness, goodness—are attitude-changing fruit. God sometimes lets us go through difficult situations to let us see what's really inside us.

An attribute is simply a personality or character trait. We call this third triplet—faith, meekness, and self-control—attribute fruit because these qualities cannot be attributed to you but only to the Holy Ghost.

Within you lies the ability to become whatever you choose to be. Remember that you have a choice, and the choice does not come without a price.

Your Thoughts

1. What's your spiritual temperature? Are you hot or cold or lukewarm? What would others say your spiritual temperature currently is?

_____

_____

_____

2. Think through the atmospheres around you at home, at work, in your ministry area, or in any of your regular endeavors. How has the Holy Spirit used love, joy, and/or peace to change the atmosphere around you in those activities?

_____

_____

_____

_____

3. How would other people assess your attitude during times of great blessing? What would they say about your attitude during times of trial? Why are longsuffering, gentleness, and goodness important to your life right now?

_____

_____

_____

_____

_____

4. Are you someone whom God would describe as bearing His character? How would you score on a report card in the subjects of faith, meekness, or self-control?

_____

_____

_____

_____

5. "Within you lies the ability to become whatever you choose to be." What does this statement mean to you personally? Why do our choices have price tags attached? What might some of these price tags be?

_____

_____

_____

_____

Meditation

"You have a strength that defies human logic. You have an ability to stand that you cannot attribute to anyone but God. You have a peace that even the apostle Paul couldn't understand, so he called it the "peace of God, which passeth all understanding" (Phil. 4:7). You have a joy that the apostle Peter could not describe, so he called it "joy unspeakable and full of glory" (I Pet. I:8)."

Have you experienced the peace that passes all understanding? Think about one of those times and thank God for His mercy and grace. Have you experienced unspeakable, glorious joy? Think about one of those times and thank God for His love and faithfulness.

DAY 30

FRUIT AND PATIENCE

Verily, verily, I say unto you, except a corn of wheat fall into the ground and die, it abideth alone: but if it die, it bringeth forth much fruit (John 12:24).

Excerpt: *Release Your Anointing*, Chapter 6.

Truth can be seen in the physical and spiritual realms. Jesus illustrated a dynamic spiritual truth with the seed example. The outer casing of a seed has only one purpose: to house the heart of the grain, which produces new life.

This outer casing is like our flesh, which houses our soul and spirit. As we "crucify the flesh" (Gal. 5:24) and "seek those things which are above" (Col. 3:1), the life of the Spirit comes to full fruition in us.

We can confidently say:

I am crucified with Christ: nevertheless I live; yet not I, but Christ liveth in me: and the life which I now live in the flesh I live by the faith of the Son of God, who loved me, and gave Himself for me (Galatians 2:20).

Your Thoughts

1. Have you died to your flesh? Are you taking steps in that direction? Is this a yearly, monthly, daily, or moment-by-moment death?

_____

_____

_____

_____

2. Will being "crucified with Christ" bring death to your flesh? How will your faith flourish if you can put to death your fleshly desires?

_____

_____

_____

_____

3. Have you known people who seem to have no problem defeating satan's temptations? Do you think they constantly rely on the Holy Ghost? Or are they falling apart from within?

_____

_____

_____

_____

4. Are you patient enough to wait for the new life to sprout from you?

_____

_____

_____

_____

_____

5. What exciting new growth have you experienced since dying to sin? Are you taking an active role in nurturing that new growth?

_____

_____

_____

_____

_____

Meditation

"Stop your Adamic nature from being the dominate force in your life.... In Numbers 17:1-8 God took something seemingly dead (Aaron's rod) and caused it to bud. You may long to function and produce.... Within every one of us is a spirit that cries out as Jacob, 'I know I am Jacob now, but within me is the desire to become Israel!'"

Producing fruit takes patience and the Holy Spirit. How delicious are fresh fruits—plump red strawberries in the spring, juicy watermelons in the summer, golden apples in the fall. Each takes time to become ripe and ready for picking. In the meantime are you feeding and nurturing your spirit, mind, and soul with the Word of God?

DAY 31

COME UP HIGHER

"After this I looked, and, behold, a door was opened in heaven: and the first voice which I heard was as it were of a trumpet talking to me; which said, Come up hither, and I will shew thee things which must be hereafter" (Revelation 4:1).

Excerpt: *Release Your Anointing,* Chapter 7.

He that hath an ear, let him hear what the Spirit saith unto the churches (Revelation 3:6).

What the Spirit reveals is totally awesome. The scope of God's blessing covers what eye has not seen and what ear has not heard. It gets even more mind-blowing than that! The storehouse of God's will for our lives includes blessings that we have never even thought about—things that surpass even our wildest imaginations; things that have never even entered our hearts. That's awesome!

But God hath revealed them unto us by His Spirit: for the Spirit searcheth all things, yea, the deep things of God (I Corinthians 2:10).

The apostle Paul calls them "the deep things of God." Many of us never get past the first oracles or the starting place with God.

The storehouse of Heaven is full. You will never exhaust its inventory of glory. If we aren't walking in such a way to access it, however, these glorious realities will never occur in our lives.

Therefore, leaving the principles of the doctrine of Christ, let us go on unto perfection (Hebrews 6:1a).

We must move away from where we first started with God.

Your Thoughts

1. Since we all have ears, what ear is Revelation 3:6 referring to? How do we hear with this ear?

_____

_____

_____

_____

2. What has the Spirit revealed to you that is totally awesome? How are can we access God's storehouse in a way that we are blessed beyond our wildest imaginations?

_____

_____

3. What do you think the "deep things of God" are? What do you think it means that the "Spirit searchest all things"?

_____

_____

_____

4. Do you feel like you have moved beyond where you started with God? In what ways have you moved forward? Have there been times when you have not moved forward the way God wanted?

_____

_____

_____

5. How do we access the storehouse of Heaven? What glory do we receive as we move beyond the basics in the Kingdom?

_____

_____

_____

_____

_____

_____

Meditation

"Many Christians never access the windows of Heaven because they are still living in the outer court and have never broken through to the third dimension, the holy of holies. Many live in defeat and carnality because they have remained on the same level where they first boarded the ark of salvation."

How well do you access the windows of Heaven? Do you feel like you regularly go to the holy of holies? Take some time to consider what God wants you to do to come up higher.

DAY 32

MESSAGES TO SEVEN CHURCHES—
Part I: Jesus in the Midst

"The mystery of the seven stars that you saw in my hand and of the seven golden lampstands is this: The seven stars are the angels of the seven churches, and the seven lampstands are the seven churches" (Revelation 1:20).

Excerpt: *Release Your Anointing*, Chapter 7.

In Revelation 2:1, Jesus walked in the midst of the church at Ephesus. In Revelation 3:20, He stands on the outside knocking for an entrance. This shows the digression of the church. Each one of these churches depicts our life as a child of God at one time or another.

1. We have left our first love (Rev. 2:4).

2. We have been crushed as the church of Smyrna, a city noted for its perfume or myrrh (Rev. 2:8).

3. We have had the spirit of Pergamos in us, which has caused others to stumble (Rev. 2:14).

4. We have things in us that were strong but now have begun to die, as is the case with the church of Sardis (Rev. 3:2).

This revelation came as a result of the seven spirits of God and seven stars. The seven spirits denote perfection or completion. It is not seven different spirits, but shows the fullness of one Spirit (Isa. 11:2). The seven stars denote the ministers. The word they preached, in conjunction with the Spirit, brought about this revelation to the churches (Rev. 1:20).

Your Thoughts

1. Why does Revelation 3:20 show the digression of the church? Why do you think the church has left Jesus out of its ministry?

_____

_____

_____

_____

2. What is "first love"? What characterizes this type of love? Is this true of you?

_____

_____

_____

3. Have you ever felt crushed like the church in Smyrna? What are some ways in which the world can crush you? What about the church or other Christians?

_____

_____

_____

4. Would the Lord ever tell you that you had caused someone to stumble? What does this mean? What do you think is at the core of influencing someone else away from the gospel?

_____

_____

_____

5. Is the accusation against the church of Sardis part of your life or someone you know? What creates a short-term Christian? Why do you think endurance is so difficult?

_____

_____

_____

_____

Meditation

"Revelation from God comes in three segments: past, present, and future. First, God sometimes reveals things in our past for instruction or edification. Jesus told the apostle John on the isle of Patmos, 'Write the things which thou hast seen [past], and the things which are [present]...Sometimes God reaches into your storm or dilemma and tells you everything will be all right. Write...the things which shall be hereafter [future]' (Rev. 1:19)."

Has God ever explained your past to you? Has He allowed you to see His perspective of the present part of your life? Has He ever explained your future? Consider what you must do to be in the place to receive revelations from the Lord.

DAY 33

MESSAGES TO SEVEN CHURCHES— Part 2: He Knows Us

"To the angel of the church in Saris write: These are the words of him who holds the seven spirits of God and the seven stars. I know your deeds; you have a reputation of being alive, but you are dead" (Revelation 3:1).

Excerpt: *Release Your Anointing*, Chapter 7.

Let's look at the message given to the churches in Revelation, chapters 2 and 3:

1. God says to the churches, "I know." These are humbling—even frightening—words. Just think of all there is to know about you. God says, "I know."

2. God says, "I know thy works." God looks beyond surface appearance and says, "I know what others do not know because I know the heart."

3. God says, "I know your name." God knows our name or reputation. Did you know that God knows your name and still loves you? He can know your reputation and still use you. He can know who you really are behind that worship, behind that song, behind that dance, behind your tongues, behind your preaching.

4. God sees beyond the name to the reality. Death means a separation, to cut off. It's like turning a light switch to the off position, which breaks the circuit and cuts off the power. God says, "I know that you are separated from life. Your name may say differently, but I know."

5. God also reveals a blessing. Something remained to work with.

Your Thoughts

1. Is it disconcerting to realize that God knows you inside and out, that every hidden place is open to Him? How can these words be frightening? How could these words be humbling?

_____

_____

_____

2. Isn't it incredible that God knows every work you have done, whether in secret or openly expressed? Since we don't need to remind Him of every good thing we have done, does it make it exciting for Him to look into your heart and your true intentions? Or does this make you feel uneasy?

_____

_____

_____

_____

3. How important is it to you to have a "good name," a reputation that shines? Are there some people who may praise you and others who may not think so highly of you? Is it comforting to know that God sees beyond what others think?

_____

_____

_____

_____

4. When people think highly of you, can you tell the difference between praise and flattery? When people criticize you, do you see the difference between the truth someone may share and the condemnation that is not of God? Why do we have to die to what others think and say?

    _____

    _____

    _____

    _____

5. After God has seen your insides, looked through your good works, peered beyond your reputation, and allowed you to die to yourself, how does He find something remaining with which He can work? What are areas of purity that He can work with inside of you?

    _____

    _____

    _____

    _____

Meditation

"God says, 'I know the truth. I know your name.' God knows that your name is Jacob but still asks, 'What is thy name?' Anytime an all-wise, all-knowing God asks a question, it isn't for His benefit. You need to confess, 'My name is Jacob.'"

Even though He knows your name, He wants you to confess it because He is going to change your name and speak a glorious destiny over you.

Think about how Jacob was before and after he wrestled with the angel. God knew his deceit and still wanted to use him. Why does Jacob's answer of telling his name help us understand how the transformation can take place for each of us?

DAY 34

MESSAGES TO SEVEN CHURCHES— Part 3: Be Watchful

Be watchful, and strengthen the things which remain, that are ready to die: for I have not found thy works perfect before God (Revelation 3:2).

Excerpt: *Release Your Anointing,* Chapter 7.

- "Be watchful." The word *watchful* means to awaken or arouse something that is at the point of dying. It isn't dead yet. If the Holy Spirit said these things that remained were ready to die, there was still a little life left.

Maybe you have felt that your ministry is dead. If you feel any kick at all, you need to be aroused and to awaken, because the movement tells you it's still alive.

- "Strengthen the things that remain." The word *strengthen* means to solidify, to establish, to set upright again; to take something that has been weakened and build it back up.

Apostle Paul said, *"Most gladly therefore will I rather glory in my infirmities, that the power of Christ may rest upon me"* (2 Cor. 12:9).

When his strength had given out and his resources were exhausted, he had no other place to turn. He could rely on no other strength but the strength that God gave him.

Your own strength is not enough, but if you will take what's left of it and give it to God, Who is more than enough, you will find Him to be sufficient.

Your Thoughts

1. Is there something in your life that is at the point of dying? When something is ready to die within us, why does the Lord ask us to be watchful?

_____

_____

_____

_____

_____

2. Have you ever felt as if you were just going through the motions in ministry or that God's grace had lifted from a once-thriving ministry? What must we do to arouse the life that still remains?

_____

_____

_____

_____

3. The phrases used to describe the word *strengthen* show what we can do when things seem to be waning. What does it take to solidify a ministry endeavor? What might be necessary in order to set a relationship or ministry upright again? What are some steps that could be used so you can build up the weakened area?

_____

_____

_____

_____

4. What does Paul mean in Second Corinthians 12:9?
    Is he a masochist? What key in this verse can turn
    around our attitude? Our perception of the chal-
    lenge? Our hope for the future? Our rationale as to
    what good the problem can create?

    _____

    _____

    _____

    _____

5. Compare and contrast your own strength with the
    strength of God. What part of solving issues is
    assigned to God? What part is assigned to you?

    _____

    _____

    _____

    _____

Meditation

"Within you are gifts, callings, and talents that have been weakened, pressed down, or held back. Your vision, dream, or desire may have been crushed. You may not have had any control over the circumstances. Perhaps your disobedience grieved the Holy Spirit. But arise, my friend! Whatever the devil did to you, he didn't complete the job. He left some strength in you."

What gifts, callings, or talents do you have that have been weakened, pressed down, or held back? Do you have visions, dreams, or desires that have been crushed? Spend time asking the Lord to forgive any disobedience in your life. Ask the Holy Spirit to build up the strength that remains within you.

DAY 35

ARISE! TIME TO TAKE INVENTORY

*And Jesus answering said, A certain man went down from Jerusalem to Jericho, and fell among thieves, which stripped him of his raiment, and wounded him, and departed, leaving him **half dead*** (Luke 10:30).

Excerpt: *Release Your Anointing,* Chapter 7.

In the parable of the Good Samaritan, Jesus said the thieves left the man "half dead." His enemies made a big mistake. They left the man with just enough life to revive. He came back to life.

God knows you are a 911 case. God knows you are in critical condition. In spite of your dilemma, He says, "It's not over until I say it's over." You may have been diagnosed with a terminal illness. Place your case in the hands of the Great Physician. Refuse to accept the verdict. Get a second opinion.

When you have healthy thoughts about your own identity, it frees you from the need to impress other people. Their opinion ceases to be the shrine where you worship! While we dress and smell nice outwardly, people do not hear the constant hammering and sawing going on inwardly as the Lord works within us, trying desperately to meet a deadline and present us as a newly constructed masterpiece fit for the Master's use.

Your Thoughts

1. Satan would love to see you say last rites over your dreams or your ministry. What can you do to stop him from achieving his goal?

   _____

   _____

   _____

2. How can you take hold of the leftovers of your life and turn them into a meal fit to serve the King?

   _____

   _____

   _____

   _____

3. The man helped by the Good Samaritan was "half dead." Do you feel as if you are half dead some days? The Holy Spirit within you is ready to breathe a big breath of fresh, pure air into your lungs—are you ready to receive it?

_____

_____

_____

4. When you take inventory of your life, do you list all of the blessings you have, or do you focus on the negative aspects of your life?

_____

_____

5. What does "God knows" mean to you?

_____

_____

_____

_____

Meditation

"You don't have to pretend. God knows everything isn't all right. God knows you aren't on top of the situation. God knows. . . .In the midst of your trial, dilemma, or storm, do you still find a desire to overcome? Do you refuse to take no for an answer? He can take everything you have lost—your time, joy, and integrity—and bring you right up to date as though it never happened."

Arise! Take inventory of your life from God's perspective. He sees you as treasure beyond compare. How does His perspective line up with yours?

DAY 36

GOD'S LAYAWAY PLAN

In whom ye also trusted, after that ye heard the word of truth, the gospel of your salvation: in whom also after that ye believed, ye were sealed with that holy Spirit of promise, which is the earnest of our inheritance until the redemption of the purchased possession, unto the praise of His glory (Ephesians 1:13-14).

Excerpt: *Release Your Anointing,* Chapter 8.

How can you keep going when all hell has been unleashed against you? If our generation will usher in the coming of the Lord—and I believe prophecy indicates we will—then we must be equipped to face the onslaught of the devil.

Paul penned the words of Ephesians, the first of his prison letters, from the confines of a Roman jail. Despite his circumstances, Paul viewed life from an eternal perspective.

The Greek word for earnest in Ephesians 1:13-14 is *arrhabon,* meaning a "pledge, a down payment, a security deposit." It's an amount paid in advance to secure the transaction until the full price is paid to complete the purchase.

If you've ever bought merchandise on layaway, you place a down payment on your goods with the promise to pay the full amount. In your case, God wants you enough that He paid earnest money to secure the transaction. When the devil offers you the world, God says, "Sorry, devil. I began the transaction, and I will finish it! I sealed it with a promise. The transaction will not be complete until I redeem the body. Until that day comes, I own all rights. This is mine."

Your Thoughts

1. Have you ever felt that all hell had been unleashed against you? What kind of preparation do we need to face onslaughts of the enemy in the future?

   _____

   _____

2. Think through Ephesians 1:13-14 and put each phrase into your own "amplified" version, personalizing what it means to you.

   _____

   _____

   _____

   _____

3. What kind of deposit has God made on your life?
    What security has He put down to seal the initial
    transaction?

    _____

    _____

    _____

    _____

4. What comfort do you have in the fact that God fin-
    ishes what He begins? How does this assurance allow
    you to focus on "running the race" rather than wor-
    rying about whether you are in the race or not?

    _____

    _____

    _____

    _____

5. When will God redeem us? Until then, does the devil have any rights to you? Do you have any rights to yourself? Why do you belong to God?

_____

_____

_____

_____

_____

Meditation

"If we see a piece of property that we want but do not have the entire price, we can put a deposit or a down payment on it. Both parties understand that a portion of the payment is still owed. This merely declares to other interested parties that the property already has a purchaser. To confirm the desire to purchase, the potential owner has given earnest money or a security deposit."

Spiritually speaking, what kind of mortgage does God have on you? Do you see yourself as a spiritual investment of God's portfolio? Pray that the Lord will open your heart to understand how much value you have to Him.

DAY 37

NOT WITHOUT A PRICE

For a just man falleth seven times, and riseth up again: but the wicked shall fall into mischief (Proverbs 24:16).

Excerpt: *Release Your Anointing*, Chapter 8.

If you ever get around people who have accomplished much, they will tell you that those accomplishments didn't come without a price. Generally, that cost is much more expensive than you normally want to pay.

The real price of success lies within the need to persevere. The trophy is never given to someone who does not complete the task. Setbacks are just set-ups for God to show what He is able to do. Funerals are for people who have accepted the thought that everything is over. Don't do that; instead, tell the enemy, "I am not dead yet."

Jesus seldom attended funerals. When He did, it was to arrest death and stop the ceremony. The Lord doesn't like pity parties, and those who have them are shocked to find that although He is invited, He seldom attends.

The whole theme of Christianity is one of rising again. However, you can't rise until you fall. That doesn't mean you should fall into sin. It means you should allow the resurrecting power of the Holy Ghost to operate in your life, regardless of whether you have fallen into sin, discouragement, apathy, or fear.

Your Thoughts

1. Have you ever thrown yourself a pity party? Did you expect Jesus to show up? Did He?

_____

_____

_____

2. What is the cost of transforming yourself into the person God wants you to be? Are you willing to pay that cost? Why?

_____

_____

_____

3. There is a certain safety in being dormant. Do you ever feel as if being dormant is better than reaching out and taking a risk? Can goals be achieved by inactivity?

_____

_____

_____

_____

4. Have you paid a high price for something you wanted and then after you got it home you quickly tired of it? Paying the cost of being God's child comes with eternal rewards—name some.

_____

_____

_____

_____

5. How hard is it to rise after a fall? Do you keep track of how many times you have had to pick yourself up? God will always soften your landing if you ask Him; He will always give you His hand to lift you up. Do you believe this truth?

_____

_____

_____

_____

Meditation

"There are obstacles that can trip you as you escalate toward productivity. But it doesn't matter what tripped you; it matters that you rise up.... Regardless of what causes us to fall, what matters it that we get up!... The Holy Spirit challenges us to stand in the midst of contrary winds, and if we stumble to our knees, to grasp the hand of God's grace and arise."

All of us will fall—it is up to us to decide whether we will rise up again. Faith will keep us dependent on His strength. Love will keep us focused on Him. Hope will give us the power to release our anointing.

DAY 38

RELENTLESS

And not only they, but ourselves also, which have the firstfruits of the Spirit, even we ourselves groan within ourselves, waiting for the adoption, to wit, the redemption of our body (Romans 8:23).

Excerpt: *Release Your Anointing*, Chapter 8.

Relentless is the word I use to describe people who will not take no for an answer. They try things one way, and if that doesn't work, they try it another way. You who are about to break beneath the stress of intense struggles, be relentless. Do not quit!

A terrible thing happens to people who give up too easily. It is called *regret*. It is the nagging, gnawing feeling that says, "If I had tried harder, I could have succeeded."

Granted, we all experience some degree of failure. That is how we learn and grow. The problem is when we fail to question if it was our lack of commitment that allowed us to forfeit an opportunity to turn the test into a triumph! We can never be sure of the answer unless we rally our talents, muster our courage, have faith and hope, and focus our strength to achieve a goal.

Many of you are near a breakthrough in your life. You may have fought for years to get to where you are with God. Many of you are pregnant with destiny. You are carrying within the womb of your spirit a ministry that could change the world.

Your Thoughts

1. Define the word *relentless* in your own words. Have you ever been relentless about a personal goal or pursuit? What gave you the drive to press ahead, no matter what?

   _____

   _____

   _____

2. When challenges occur, how do relentless people react? How does the process of trial and error produce innovations and stronger people? Do you react to challenges with a relentless spirit?

   _____

   _____

   _____

3. Have you any regrets about your life thus far? What has created those regrets? How can you prevent future regrets?

_____

_____

_____

_____

4. What are some things that you have tried and failed? How did you feel about those failures? Were they easy to accept? Have you ever been able to turn a failure into a triumph? What made the difference?

_____

_____

_____

_____

5. Since we do not know the future, we could be on the edge of a breakthrough and not know it. How does this possibility motivate us to move forward in a storm?

_____

_____

_____

_____

Meditation

"We must understand the working of the Holy Spirit. Many become discouraged when they fall short of their goals as a child of God."

The spirit is saved by faith, and the body is saved by hope. Hope purifies our soul. When it doesn't look good, hope says, "It's all right." This is why we need a strong witness in our soul. God gives us hope in the midst of our storm.

How is your spirit saved by faith? How is your body saved by hope? Pray that the Lord increases your faith and your hope. Receive the comfort and peace that only the Lord can provide.

DAY 39

GOD INHABITS
AN OLD HOUSE

But I keep under my body, and bring it into subjection: lest that by any means, when I have preached to others, I myself should be a castaway (1 Corinthians 9:27).

Excerpt: *Release Your Anointing*, Chapter 8.

Within our decaying shells, we constantly peel away, by faith, the lusts and jealousies that adorn the walls of our hearts. If the angels were to stroll through the earth with the Creator and ask, "Which house is Yours?" He would pass by all the mansions and cathedrals. Unashamedly, He would point at you and me and say, "That is Mine!" We who blunder and stumble in our humanity continually wrestle with the knowledge that *our God has put so much in so little!*

Despite all our washing and painting, all our grooming and exercising, this old house is still falling apart. There is no doubt that we have been saved, and there is no doubt that *the house is haunted.* The Holy Ghost Himself resides beneath this sagging roof.

This divine occupation is not an act of a desperate guest who, having no place else to stay, chose this impoverished site as a temporary place to "ride out" the storm. No, God Himself has—of His own free will and predetermined purpose—put us in the embarrassing situation of entertaining a Guest whose lofty stature so far exceeds us that we hardly know how to serve Him!

Your Thoughts

1. Why do you think God has chosen our rickety shells in which to house His Spirit? What does this show about God's love for humanity?

   _____

   _____

   _____

2. How does One who is so perfect live in squalor within our dying frame? Does this knowledge humble you? Do you receive encouragement by knowing that within you resides Someone who can outperform anyone on earth?

   _____

   _____

   _____

3. Are there surface areas in your life that you have attempted to whitewash and secure, while something was rotting underneath? Think through this question carefully. Let God reveal what you may have tried to cover without addressing the root cause.

_____

_____

_____

_____

4. How should we "take care" of our Guest? What should we do to serve Him?

_____

_____

_____

_____

5. How would you explain the indwelling of the Holy
    Spirit to a new Christian? What impact has the Spirit
    made on your life so you can give testimony first-
    hand as to His occupation in your temple?

    _____

    _____

    _____

    _____

    _____

Meditation

"I pay very little attention to those among us who feel obligat-
ed to impress us with the ludicrous idea that they have already
attained what is meant to be a lifelong pursuit. The renewal of the
old person is a daily exercise of the heart. It progressively strength-
ens the character day by day, not overnight!"

Have you ever met someone who thought they had already
attained their lifelong pursuit? Do these kinds of people continue
to grow past the place where they think they have "arrived?" What
do we need to do to keep a teachable spirit so we continually grow
toward God's future for us?

DAY 40

STRIPPED DOWN
TO THE ETERNAL

So He got up from the meal, took off His outer clothing, and wrapped a towel around His waist (John 13:4).

Excerpt: *Release Your Anointing*, Chapter 8.

Jesus laid aside His garments. That is what ministry is all about. It requires you to lay aside your garments. Lay aside your personal ambitions. Ministry is birthed when you are stripped down to your heart's desire, when beneath every other thread of whimsical grandeur, your heart says, I want my life to have counted for something. *I want to accomplish something for God.*

Have you ever prayed, "Oh God, don't let me impress anyone else but the One to whom I gave my life"?

Have we given our lives to the Lord? Then why are we still standing around the table arguing over who is going to sit on the left and who is going to sit on the right? *Why have we not laid aside our garments?*

You can never be really anointed until you personally experience a situation that calls you to lay aside your garments. It is from this that the tears of worship are born. They fall lavishly down a face that has been pulled from behind its covering and laid bare before God. Who can help but worship Him, once we see Him aside from every distraction and weight?

Your Thoughts

1. If you had been with the disciples when Jesus began to wash their feet, how do you think you would have reacted? Would you have been embarrassed or confused? Would our reactions have been different from the disciples?

_____

_____

_____

_____

_____

_____

2. How much do you want your life to count for in the Kingdom? How greatly do you desire to do something for God? Are you willing to set aside what you think this means, and listen to what God thinks?

_____

_____

_____

_____

_____

3. When we give our lives over to the Lord, what kind of ownership decision have we made in terms of our bodies, souls, and spirits? What rights does the Owner have over us? Do we have any rights?

_____

_____

_____

_____

4. Why is *anointed* so connected with *humility* in service? Why are these paramount to a deeper anointing?

_____

_____

_____

_____

_____

_____

5. How does worship affect your life? Do you ever find yourself naked and laid bare before the Lord during worship? Is this important so we can see God clearly and commune with Him face to face?

_____

_____

_____

_____

_____

Meditation

"The garment represents different things to different people. It is whatever camouflages our realness, whatever hinders us from really affecting our environment. Our garments are the personal agendas that we have set for ourselves. Like the fig leaves sewn together in the garden, we have contrived our own coverings. The terrible tragedy of it all is that soon or later, whatever we have sown together will ultimately be stripped away."

What garments are you currently wearing that need to be laid aside so you can serve God? What agendas do you need to put on hold? How will God honor your service to Him?

THOUGHTS & REFLECTIONS

_____

_____

_____

_____

_____

_____

_____

_____

_____

_____

_____

_____

_____

_____

_____

_____

_____

_____

_____

_____

_____

_____

_____

_____

_____

_____

_____

_____

_____

_____

_____

_____

_____

_____

_____

_____

_____

_____

_____

_____

_____

_____

_____

_____

_____

_____

_____

_____

_____

_____

_____

_____

_____

_____

_____

_____

_____

_____

_____

_____

_____

Additional copies of this book and other
book titles from DESTINY IMAGE are
available at your local bookstore.

Call toll-free: 1-800-722-6774.

Send a request for a catalog to:

Destiny Image® Publishers, Inc.
P.O. Box 310
Shippensburg, PA 17257-0310

*"Speaking to the Purposes of God for This
Generation and for the Generations to Come."*

**For a complete list of our titles,
visit us at www.destinyimage.com.**